IMAGES
of America

FORT STORY
and CAPE HENRY

Suki and David—
Just to remind you
of home.

Enjoy!

Fielding L. Tyler

December 2005

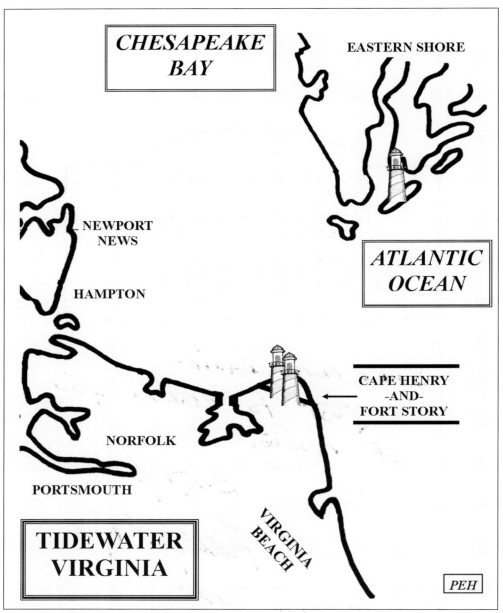

The Tidewater region of southeastern Virginia consists of low-lying land draining into the Chesapeake Bay by tidal estuaries. It stretches from Williamsburg east to the Eastern Shore of Virginia, south to Virginia Beach, and west to Southampton County. The land of Tidewater was first claimed by James I as absolutely as if had been his own by ancestral heritage. Initially no rights were given to the Native Americans who occupied the ground. The title was vested in the London Company. In the 400 years since the first landing of the English settlers, the area has dramatically grown and increased in prosperity; however, it still maintains a level of charm and a true sense of history. In its center are the protected and deepwater ports of Hampton Roads, which form the pulse of the economy, so some call the region Hampton Roads, and others refer to it as Tidewater. Both designations have historic roots.

IMAGES
of America

FORT STORY
and CAPE HENRY

Fielding Lewis Tyler

Published by Arcadia Publishing
Charleston SC, Chicago IL, Portsmouth NH, San Francisco CA

Printed in Great Britain

Library of Congress Catalog Card Number: 2005922732

For all general information contact Arcadia Publishing at:
Telephone 843-853-2070
Fax 843-853-0044
E-mail sales@arcadiapublishing.com
For customer service and orders:
Toll-Free 1-888-313-2665

Visit us on the internet at http://www.arcadiapublishing.com

June 10, 1941, was Media Day for the guns at Fort Story, Virginia. Over 500 spectators, including photographers, print and newsreel media, and military officials, watched as the troops fired service practice with all of the types of weapons at Fort Story. The biggest draws were the 16-inch howitzers fired by the blue denim–clad artillerymen at Battery Walke in their first service practice since 1928. Other soldiers from the 246th Coast Artillery Regiment fired 75-mm guns, 155-mm artillery pieces, and even the obsolete 8-inch railway guns. Joining in the practice was the 71st Coast Artillery Regiment firing its full range of weapons, from the 3-inch guns to the 37-mm antiaircraft and .50-caliber machine guns. Six months later, following the report of the attack on Pearl Harbor, a radio message was received from Fort Monroe, and within a matter of hours the harbor defenses went to full alert. The war had begun.

CONTENTS

ACKNOWLEDGMENTS

This project is respectfully dedicated to Richard "Dick" Weinert Jr. and Olivia "Libby" Alfriend. Dick served as deputy command historian at the U.S. Army Training and Doctrine Command at Fort Monroe and was both a mentor and a true friend. Libby Alfriend was also a longtime friend and served for many years as the public affairs officer at Fort Story. Without the assistance of both of these dedicated professionals, I would have never put pen to paper.

My real inspiration came from my wife, Mary Christian Sallé Tyler, who grew up at the North End of Virginia Beach and was my high-school sweetheart. She and her brothers and sister would ride the rope swings from the large sand dunes over the cypress swamps in the state park. The North End and state park were her backyard. On the post, she would go to the movies and chat with the Italian prisoners towards the end of World War II. Growing up near Cape Henry was a grand experience for a lot of children.

I have been fortunate to have a number of friends who have stepped up to the plate and helped me with gathering information for this project. The first is Julie J. Pouliot, administrator of the Old Coast Guard Station. She also serves as museum registrar and in that capacity oversees an extensive collection of local photographs. She also was a great help in scanning the images into my new Macintosh G5. Bob Zink, a distinguished historian in the field of coast artillery, generously furnished me plans and maps of the guns of Fort Story, in addition to some much needed advice. Patrick Evans-Hylton has published a number of books with Arcadia Publishing. I provided him a number of old pictures and now he owes me one. Another Arcadia author, Al Chewning, also assisted me in obtaining images of Cape Henry. At First Landing State Park, District Manager Fred Hazelwood has guided me through a pile of information on the history of the park and its role today. Mary Reid Barrow, correspondent for the *Virginia Beach Beacon*, supplement to *The Virginian-Pilot*, has been a gem in her research on both Cape Henry and First Landing State Park. Her insight has been remarkable. A snappy salute goes to Ed Amburn, who lived at Fort Story while his father was there as a coast artillery soldier. His remarkable power of recollection was a great help in preparing my text. Oliver Perry, chief emeritus of the Nansemond tribe, was very helpful in telling the story of the Chesapeake Indians in the Cape Henry area.

Throughout my project, the U.S. Army has always been helpful in assisting with obtaining information on their role at Cape Henry over the years. The garrison commander, Lt. Col. Wesley Rehorn, and his staff, specifically Sue Renner, Natalie Granger, and Sam Hartman, have gone the extra mile in assisting me in my research.

INTRODUCTION

When the ships of the English settlers entered Chesapeake Bay at dawn on the "six and twentieth day of April" in 1607, one of the landing party mentioned the fair meadows and tall trees with fresh water. They also commented on the oysters, which they found large and delicate in taste. After exploring the area, the men of the first landing were attacked by native warriors as they returned to the boat that brought them ashore. After other forays, the colonists went ashore and erected a wooden cross, naming that place Cape Henry in honor of Henry, Prince of Wales. The vessels then continued on to Jamestown. In 1791, the federal government began construction, and by October of the following year, the oil-burning lamps of the Cape Henry lighthouse were lit, proving a beacon at the entrance to Chesapeake Bay. During the War of 1812, war came to Cape Henry for a few brief periods. British Royal Marines came ashore in 1813 as a watering party. During the War between the States, local militia came to Cape Henry and damaged the light to prevent its use by ships.

In 1874, the United States Life-Saving Service built a facility to assist in rescue efforts at Cape Henry. In 1881, the second lighthouse was erected to replace the earlier lighthouse. The federal government also built a weather station adjacent to the "new" lighthouse. With the arrival of the railroad in 1902, Cape Henry became a real community. Residences and hotels began to spring up. In 1914, the federal government arrived and acquired land "to erect fortifications and for other military purposes." The army named the post Fort Story and built facilities to support two gun batteries located in the dune line. War did not come to Fort Story, and the post was reduced to caretaker status. During that period, the establishment of a state park adjacent to Fort Story became a reality; Seashore State Park opened in 1936. With the approach of World War II, the army acquired additional land and began to modernize the defenses at Cape Henry. The guns were never fired in anger, and following hostilities, the Army Transportation Corps changed the mission from artillery to army amphibians. With the phase-out of amphibious vehicles, the mission was changed to training for over-the-beach exercises as well as joint special operations.

My interest in Fort Story and Cape Henry began when, as a young man in the years following World War II, my friends and I roamed the beaches and dunes of both the army post and the North End of Virginia Beach. On occasion, our travels would take us under the fence and into the former coast artillery positions. I was fascinated by the silent guns and the concrete casemates. Using my Kodak Brownie camera, I managed to photograph a number of the camouflage structures. I certainly wish that I had done more, as a lot of history went unrecorded, but at that time my mind was on other things.

After my retirement from the U.S. Army after serving for 30 years, I returned to Virginia Beach and my interest in Cape Henry and Fort Story was rekindled. I began to assemble all of my notes and images and decided it was time to put it all together. The work has progressed through four Macintosh computer upgrades and an uneasy transfer of a number of discs and zip drives. And here we are.

Cape Henry and Fort Story are fascinating places both to the locals and to the many visitors to Virginia Beach. Our visitors marvel at the view of historic Cape Henry from the top of the Old Cape Henry Lighthouse. They enjoy the wide beaches of the North End of Virginia Beach. Visitors to First Landing State Park are given the opportunity to hike, bike, swim, fish, boat, camp, and picnic. The story of the lighthouses and the first landing in 1607 has been told a number of times. The military has only been given a brief visit. With the 400th anniversary of the landing of the English settlers at Cape Henry and their voyage on up to Jamestown, it is time to tell the story of this beautiful and historic piece of America. The time has come. Enjoy.

One

FOOTPRINTS IN THE SAND

There were footprints left in the sands of Cape Henry for many hundreds of years before the English settlers landed in 1607. They continue today with prints of sandals of visitors to First Landing State Park and boot prints of soldiers stationed on the army post at Fort Story. One hundred forty million years ago, the shoreline of Virginia was submerged beneath the Atlantic Ocean. Volcanic action, glacial movement, and continental drift have caused the land to rise to great heights and sink to the depths of the sea over the years. The Pleistocene Ice Age began about two million years ago. As the ice sheets advanced and receded, the flood plain of the Susquehanna River formed the outline of the Chesapeake Bay. As ice sheets from the last major ice age melted, the seas rose and the bay was formed. Cape Henry began as a large spit of sand deposited by ocean and river currents.

The beaches, dunes, and wooded areas of Cape Henry are as wondrous today as they were in 1607. The area was once referred to as the "Desert" for the massive moving sand dunes on the tip of the cape. The influence of the Gulf Stream and the warming trend from the south help make Cape Henry a botanically rich area. Animal species include gray squirrel, rabbits, red fox, and snakes, in addition to owls, osprey, and even a bobcat or two. It is the northernmost range for Spanish moss, which thrives in First Landing State Park. In the early years, fishermen worked in the area, designated for common use by the state. Later the State of Virginia deeded much of the land, which was defined as "a course from the mouth of Lynnhaven Bay—going 5 1/2 miles to the Atlantic Ocean to Rainey's Pond (Crystal Lake) to gut connects with Linkhorn Bay—then along gut by Linkhorn Bay to the narrows—into Broad Bay to Long Creek then along Long Creek and Lynnhaven to the beginning." The live oaks are plentiful at Cape Henry and along Shore Drive (Route 60) through First Landing State Park and the adjacent Cape Story by the Sea community. Legend has it that pirates made good use of the many inland waterways from Little Creek to the vicinity of Broad Bay and the tributaries. Legend also talks of sites where pirates buried their treasure near the waterways surrounding First Landing State Park.

The Chesapeake Indians inhabited areas from the Atlantic Ocean to the Elizabeth River until the early 17th century. They lived a mobile lifestyle and spoke a Powhatan dialect of the Algonquin language. After their disappearance, their lands were taken over by the Nansemond tribe. Here are chiefs from the Nansemond, Mataponi, Chicahominy, and Monacan tribes at a 1987 ceremony held for the reburial of 64 Chesapeake Indians. (Photograph by Tony Belcastro.)

In the 1970s and 1980s, the remains of 64 Chesapeake Indians were unearthed in the Great Neck area of Virginia Beach. The remains were housed with the Virginia Department of Historic Resources until the present-day Nansemond tribe adopted the remains and reburied them in First Landing State Park in a simple ceremony. The burial site is circular to represent all stages of man's existence. (Photograph by Tony Belcastro.)

In February 1607, 105 men, all employees of the London Company, left England en route to North America. On April 26, 1607, the three vessels entered the Chesapeake Bay and landed on the shoreline in a small shallop boat. Over a four-day period, a number of the men investigated the meadows and trees and tasted the plump strawberries and large oysters. On the fourth day, they set up a wooden cross at the newly named Cape Henry in honor of the Prince of Wales. On the opposite side of the Chesapeake, they named the land Cape Charles for Henry's brother. At the end of the first day, the Englishmen were attacked by members of the Chesapeake Indian tribe, and two members of the landing party were wounded by arrows. They then departed Cape Henry and sailed into the Chesapeake Bay and on to Jamestown. These men were certainly not the first adventurers to come to the Chesapeake Bay. There is evidence of numerous expeditions by the Spanish prior to 1607. (Drawing by Constance Fahey.)

Cape Henry, Virginia, was named for Henry Frederick Stuart, the first child of King James I of England and Anne of Denmark. Henry was born on February 19, 1594, in Scotland. He was the pride of his parents, and the heir apparent was groomed for kingship from the beginning. Henry was designated as the Prince of Wales at Westminster in June 1610. He was an accomplished swordsman, was well read, and was a true patron of the arts. The dreams of a nation were shattered in November 1612 when Henry suddenly took ill and died. It is presumed that his cause of death was typhoid fever. He was very fond of his younger sister Elizabeth, and it is said that his last words were "where is my dear sister?" A national period of mourning followed his death. (Courtesy National Portrait Gallery, London.)

Prior to the erection of the granite cross at Cape Henry in 1935, a number of anniversary ceremonies were held with a wooden cross. This is the ceremony held on April 26, 1928, at the base of the old Cape Henry Lighthouse. Virginia governor Harry Flood Byrd is the speaker. The soldiers are from the 12th Coast Artillery Regiment.

This image shows another anniversary ceremony at the wooden cross at Cape Henry. President and Mrs. Hoover attended the ceremony in April 1931. They arrived by train and joined a crowd of more than 10,000 people who had also traveled to the site. In the middle of the opening prayer, the heavens opened up and the program was quickly brought to a close. The president's hatless head was drenched, and Mrs. Hoover's blue straw hat was soaked.

The first idea of a permanent memorial cross was first mentioned at a meeting of the Daughters of the American Colonists at the home of Mrs. James Branch Cabell in Richmond. The Assembly of Tidewater Virginia Women was contacted to look into the possibility of erecting a cross. This wooden cross was placed at the site by Lawson and Newton, a monument firm, marking the site for the permanent cross. (Courtesy James A. Lawson III.)

Lawson and Newton, "The Monument People," was the monument firm selected to design and build the cross. The firm had been in business since 1903 at Eleventh Street and Monticello Avenue in Norfolk. The cross, base, patio, and wall were designed by James A. Lawson Jr., the son of company owner James A. Lawson Sr. (Courtesy James A. Lawson III.)

The base for the cross was Georgia granite delivered to Cape Henry in 1934 by the Lawson and Newton trucks. In this 1934 photograph, Miss Helen Cox of Norfolk stands atop the base in her imitation of the Statue of Liberty. Miss Cox and her family often made day trips to Cape Henry. (Courtesy Kathryn Fisher.)

A wooden cross was on the location in 1934 until the permanent cross was erected in 1935. Lawson and Newton made the actual cross in their Norfolk facility from granite from Mount Airy, North Carolina. The base was granite from Georgia. The patio slate was fieldstone brought in from Buckingham, Virginia. The materials were trucked from Norfolk and assembled on site by the Lawson and Newton crew. (Courtesy James A. Lawson III.)

The beaches at the Cape Henry Memorial Cross served as a venue for annual ceremonies for many years. Each year the beach eroded, until in 1981 it reached within 30 feet of the cross. The decision was made to relocate the cross off the beach some 200 yards to the west. Through a combined effort of the National Park Service, the City of Virginia Beach, and the U.S. Army, it was relocated in November 1981.

The army continued to build up the beach, but the National Park Service deemed that the cross and pavilion needed to be moved. The cross was picked up and relocated with a crane from the 549th Quartermaster Company, a unit of the 11th Transportation Battalion stationed at Fort Story. Other soldiers from the battalion assisted in landscaping.

The cross was first dedicated on Friday, April 26, 1935, by the national president of the National Society Daughters of the American Colonists, Mrs. Joseph Starke Calfee. The tablet marker reads, "Here at Cape Henry first landed in America, upon 26 April 1607, those English Colonists who, upon 13 May 1607, established at Jamestown, Virginia, the first permanent English settlement in America."

Cape Henry Day was celebrated in April 1947. Among the dignitaries was the Right Reverend William A. Brown, bishop of the Episcopal Diocese of Southern Virginia (in vestment, front row, second from left); and the Reverend George Purnell Gunn of the Church of the Good Shepherd in Norfolk, Virginia (in vestment, front row, second from right).

On September 5, 1781, off Cape Henry, a French fleet commanded by Adm. Francois Joseph Paul Comte de Grasse defeated a British fleet commanded by Adm. Thomas Graves. At Yorktown, General Cornwallis was awaiting the arrival of the fleet with much-needed troops and supplies. With the French victory in the Battle of the Capes, Cornwallis was denied support and the result was his surrender to Washington in October 1781.

In 1976, the Virginia Beach Bicentennial Commission brought attention to the significance of the Battle of the Capes by erecting a statue of Admiral de Grasse and constructing an overlook, from which visitors can view the Chesapeake Bay and the site of the naval engagement. The enclosed overlook has since been demolished, but a wooden ramp leads the visitor to an open overlook with signage and a clear water view.

In April 1957, the 350th-Anniversary Reenactment of the First Landing at Cape Henry was conducted on the beaches at Fort Story. In this photo on the left is Capt. Bartholomew Gosnold, portrayed by R. G. Bosher of Virginia Beach. On the right is Capt. John Smith, portrayed by E. Ashley Haycox, also of Virginia Beach. In April 2007, the 400th anniversary will again be celebrated on the beaches at Cape Henry.

The 350th-Anniversary Reenactment in 1957 brought original ship replicas to Cape Henry as part as the anniversary. The ships later sailed on to Jamestown. Notice the aircraft carrier in the left background. From left to right are Richard Minnick as Capt. John Martin, R. G. Bosher as Bartholomew Gosnold, and Eugene Gordman as Thomas Webb.

Two

GUIDING THE WAY
AT THE CAPE

By the turn of the 19th century, the Desert at Cape Henry was still a desolate place to work and raise a family. Here Dr. Corydon Cronk of the weather bureau poses for the camera with his family in their finest clothing. Cape Henry occupies one of the most beautiful pieces of coastal property in the entire Commonwealth of Virginia. Located at the confluence of the Chesapeake Bay and the Atlantic Ocean, it offers views of the most scenic ocean and bay water and is surrounded by centuries-old live oaks and sand dunes. An important piece of its history is the two lighthouses. The first became operational in October 1792 and remained active for over 100 years. It was replaced by the "new" lighthouse, which was erected during the period 1879–1881. The combination of lighthouses, life-saving stations, and the Virginia Pilots have guided and assisted many a mariner from the earliest days as they enter and exit the waters of the Chesapeake Bay.

The "old" Cape Henry Lighthouse is currently owned and maintained by the Association for the Preservation of Virginia Antiquities (APVA). The lighthouse is in the center of the official seal of the city of Virginia Beach. In 1792, it was a lonely life for the keeper and his family, and except for fishermen, no other humans lived on the sands of Cape Henry.

This is the "new" Cape Henry lighthouse shortly after it became operational. The tower was built with prefabricated cast-steel plates on a masonry foundation. The first-order Fresnel lens in the lantern room has a range of 19 miles. Today the original 1881 Fresnel lamp is still in place, providing light to mariners as it has for well over 100 years.

In this 1898 photograph, the children of the men stationed at Cape Henry in the lighthouse, the weather bureau, and the life-saving station pose before the "old" Cape Henry Lighthouse. From left to right are Elwood Midgett, Harold Howell, Don Cronk, Maggie Midgett, Edith Midgett, and Will Midgett (in the wheelbarrow). The children played on the large dunes and peered down on the trees in the cypress swamp beyond.

One of the men assigned to the Cape Henry Lighthouse poses outside the watch room in 1915. In the background is the Hygeia Hotel, as well as a number of the large cottages on the beach. The members of the life-saving service lived in smaller houses with their families when they were not on duty. At 163 feet, the new lighthouse is the tallest cast-iron tower in the United States.

The original fog signal building was built in 1881 and was operated by steam. Reports in 1901 indicate the signal consumed about 17 tons of coal, and water was obtained from an adjacent cistern. By 1909, the signal was operated by oil-fired compressed air. A reinforced fog signal–testing laboratory was completed in 1935. Newly arrived soldiers at Fort Story "came straight up in their beds" when the fog horn first sounded.

This 1944 photograph shows the lighthouse compound. Two years earlier, German U-boat captain Horst Degen guided the U-701 to Cape Henry using the beacon from this light as well as the lighthouse at Cape Charles. The army occupied the watch room and used it as an artillery battery commander's station. The tower to the right of the lighthouse is an early army radar used to track targets for the coastal artillery.

By 1890, all lighthouses in the United States were using kerosene. The volatile nature of kerosene required the construction of separate oil houses. When oil was no longer required, the structures were used for paint storage. The brick oil house at Cape Henry was built in 1892 with a capacity of 500 gallons. This building today retains its original ventilation hood and pipes.

On the light station, there were quarters for a keeper and two assistant keepers. This first assistant keeper's quarters were completed after the tower was erected. It was built on brick piers with brick chimneys and originally had clapboard siding. The gable ends were covered with decorative board and batten and gingerbread. The roof was originally wood shingle. The quarters today have been covered with siding and are no longer occupied.

The second assistant keeper's quarters were built after the tower was erected and are similar in design to the first assistant quarters. During the 1930s, these quarters were occupied by Mr. I. C. Midgett. Under the management of the U.S. Coast Guard, the quarters were designated as Quarters C. They are still on the compound today and are presently unoccupied.

This is the third of the original set of quarters built on the lighthouse compound. In the late 1930s, it was occupied by the family of Assistant Keeper Utah C. Jennette. Recent research indicates that in 1938, for whatever reason, the building was relocated off the grounds adjacent to Atlantic Avenue on Fort Story. It is currently in use by the U.S. Army and designated as Quarters 711.

This 1944 photograph depicts is the newest building on the light station. Built in 1938, it again provided three sets of quarters. It served as the keepers' quarters and was designated as Quarters A. It remained in use by the U.S. Coast Guard until 1999, when the last crew was reassigned, thus ending the 118-year tradition as a manned station. This substantial brick building remains.

The Virginia Pilot Association was formed in 1866. Since that time, the pilots have been responsible guardians of the entrance to Hampton Roads. The first boat stationed off Cape Henry was a wooden schooner, and it was later followed by steam-powered vessels. In this late-1950s photograph, a yawl boat is being lowered to pick up the pilots off the beach at Fort Story. (Courtesy Virginia Pilot Association.)

A yawl boat delivers passengers from the pilot boat launch off Cape Henry to the beach in the 1930s. These sturdy yawl boats carried pilots, supplies, mail, and visitors to and from the beach. The Virginia Pilot Association continues to provide pilotage service to both U.S. and foreign vessels that call at the ports of the bay. It has insured the well-being of our local ports in both peace and war.

In July 1983, the pilot boat *Virginia III* got underway, leaving the station for the final time. A new era in efficiency was underway. At Lynnhaven Inlet, a new dormitory and maintenance facility was built. The communications building at Cape Henry tracks vessels entering the port. Using these "50-footers," the age-old practice of meeting incoming vessels and guiding them safely into port has not changed. (Courtesy Virginia Pilot Association.)

Three

The Weather Service and the Emerging Community

The weather station was first established in a one-story signal service building in December 1873. The station served as the residence of Dr. Corydon Cronk from 1898 until 1903. He had moved his family and all their belongings on a boat from Baltimore to Norfolk, then onto the railroad to Virginia Beach. In 1870, Congress signed a law providing for the taking of meteorological observations using the assets of the U.S. Army Signal Service (later Signal Corps). The signal service began issuing weather bulletins and in 1874 set up operations at Cape Henry. A telegraph line was completed from Norfolk to Cape Henry and down the beach to Cape Hatteras. In 1891, the duties performed by the army were transferred to the newly established weather bureau. At Cape Henry, the weather bureau set up business in a wooden building and relocated to a permanent building until it closed in 1969. In 1890, the Cape Henry Park and Land Company was chartered to acquire Cape Henry for development and timber interests.

This is a 1901 photograph of the new weather bureau building. It served as the office and residence of the Cronk family from 1901 to 1903. In these days, a barometer, thermometer, anemometer, and a rain gauge were all the tools a meteorologist required. Balloons, radar, and satellites are part of the array that weather watchers use today. Instruments from the old building are on display at the Old Coast Guard Station.

Dr. Corydon P. Cronk was assigned to the U.S. Weather Bureau Station in February 1898. He moved from Baltimore to Cape Henry. Cronk had married Carrie Patten, and the couple had a son, Corydon "Don" Patten Cronk, born in 1887. This 1902 photograph shows a portion of the family music and dining rooms.

This 1898 photograph is titled "Don's tent at Cape Henry, Virginia, August 1898." From left to right are Helen Ethridge, Don Cronk, and Watson Ethridge. Don Cronk writes that "right behind my house there are large sand hills that cover the tops of trees. The boys go over there and jump all the way down. I see very many boats, some of them are battleships and some torpedo boats."

In this 1898 photograph, the youngsters at Cape Henry are ready to repel a Spanish invasion. This was the period of the Spanish-American War, and our crew is armed with a hoe, several brooms, and a couple of bows. Taking cover behind a sand fort, from left to right, are Edith Midgett, Elwood Rowden, Perry Howell, Don Cronk, Harold Howell, Maggie Midgett, and Will Midgett.

Carrie P. Cronk among the myrtle bushes at Cape Henry.
1900

The photograph is titled "Carrie P. Cronk among the myrtle bushes at Cape Henry 1900." Carrie had to travel seven miles down the beach to obtain provisions to feed her family. After a year, the family purchased a cow, and they shared the milk with the neighbors. At that time, hogs ran wild on the beaches and dunes. They served the purpose of keeping the beaches free of garbage and residue from the fish nets.

In this 1898 photograph, Don Cronk (left) and his friends display fish taken after hauling in a seine. Don describes the haul as "about 1200 trout of immense size." Fish were a staple of the diet at Cape Henry. They were usually cooked immediately after catching and salted down for use in the winter. A number of families got together and jointly owned a 100-yard seine net.

This August 12, 1885, photograph is titled "Leaving Cape Henry Light Station." Neither the ladies in the cart nor the individuals on the porch of the house are identified. The house in the background is quarters for one of the keepers. The wide-track wheels on the cart enable it to maneuver in the soft sand. Trips down the beach were usually made at low tide on the hard sand closer to the water.

In 1918, a new "three story and a cellar" brick observatory building was erected by the Department of Agriculture to house the weather station at Cape Henry. The architect was Mr. Frank Upman of Washington, D.C. During World War II, the military used the building as a Harbor Entrance Control Point. Mr. Clement R. White served as bureau chief from 1933 until 1953. The station was closed in May 1969.

In 1902, the first railroad tracks were laid to Cape Henry by the Chesapeake Transit Company. This electric "North Shore" route extended from Norfolk east across the 2,200-foot railway trestle at Lynnhaven Inlet on to Cape Henry. Norfolk Southern began to expand their services northward from Virginia Beach with steam trains. For two years, there were parallel rail lines, one electric and one steam.

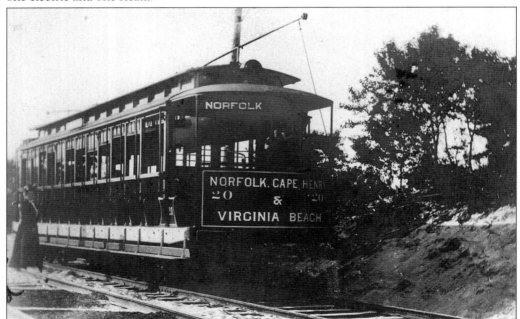

This 1903 photograph is titled "one of the first trolley cars at Cape Henry." By June of the following year, the Chesapeake Transit Company was taken over by Norfolk Southern. The steam line was abandoned and dismantled. The establishment of rail service was important to the economy. There was now access to the cape other than riding the beach in a buggy.

The brick and granite church designated as St. Theresa's Chapel was dedicated in October 1924. Construction of the church was sponsored by the Reverend Philip P. Brennan of the Star of the Sea Catholic Church in Virginia Beach. Prior to World War II, the chapel closed down, and it did not reopen until after the war, when it was renovated by the army, which had taken over the land.

Pictured here is the large house of Assistant Lighthouse Keeper Albert Midgett. Midgett bought about a city block of land to the west of the lighthouse and built this house sometime before 1890. When Albert Midgett retired from the Coast Guard, he stayed in his house and opened a small store and gas station at the corner of 141st Street and Atlantic Avenue. Midgett sold a lot of ice cream.

Following the Hurricane of 1933, Mr. Allen Willett of Princess Anne County began to build a permanent summer residence on the west side of Atlantic Avenue. The structure would replace an oceanfront cottage damaged by the hurricane. The army condemned the property prior to World War II, and the house was never completed. Today it is occupied by the Directorate of Public Works at Fort Story.

Summer at Cape Henry in the early 1930s was a magical time and place. These children are in front of a beach cottage on 145th Street on the oceanfront. They could walk four blocks south and buy ice cream at Midgett's store. From left to right are John Horchner, Louise Horchner, Billy Underwood, and Dick Horchner.

This postcard depicts the 1903 train station at Cape Henry. It was central to the small community that was beginning to grow. The post office opened in this building; Mr. Doc Washburn served as the first postmaster in addition to being the stationmaster/ticket taker and running a concession. Washburn was proprietor of the Seabreeze Hotel across the street and operated a store on the first floor.

Here is a little problem with a truck stuck on the tracks in 1949. The rail line to Cape Henry ran up Pacific Avenue on the oceanfront and parallel to Atlantic Avenue, north to Fort Story and through the post. The line then extended through what are now First Landing State Park and the community of Cape Story by the Sea. It then crossed the Lynnhaven Inlet and went to Norfolk.

The Norfolk Southern Railroad ran passenger service from Norfolk to Virginia Beach to Cape Henry and back to Norfolk. Starting at Cape Henry, students from W. T. Cooke Elementary and Oceana High School boarded at stations or streets on Atlantic Avenue and rode to the station at Seventeenth Street. Depicted is Number 103, "The Cavalier," which went into service in 1935. The service was discontinued in November 1947.

William O'Keefe was originally from Norfolk and was in the dry cleaning business. He moved to Virginia Beach and loved to walk on the beach at Cape Henry. He decided to build a casino at that location and opened O'Keefe's Casino in 1904. By this time, the rail line extended to Cape Henry and the facility drew large crowds. From the best accounts, the casino closed in 1931 and the building burned down the following year.

In 1902, the Cape Henry Park and Land Company was reorganized as the Cape Henry Syndicate, which sold parcels of land on their property on the west of the post at Fort Story. A large number of individuals purchased lots and some built summer cottages. Prior to World War II, this large single-story structure was used at one time as a girls' camp.

This is another house erected on property purchased from the Cape Henry Syndicate. These dwellings in some instances were permanent residences and in others were summer cottages. This house was located next to the railroad near the train station. This and other buildings were condemned by the army when the installation was expanded. They served for many years as military family housing.

Erosion at Cape Henry has been a consistent problem. Over the years, the army has put everything from surplus DUKW amphibious vehicles to rocks to large, sand-filled geotubes on the beach to stem the encroaching water. This image is taken following the Ash Wednesday storm of March 1962. The weather-bureau building withstood the storm with a concrete wall and large rip rap along the beach. In 1998, three back-to-back storms breached the dunes. The dunes were restored, but the beach erosion continued. As a result of that damage, the army contracted in 2002 to have 18 stone breakwaters built along a mile of the beach from the south to this building. The breakwater is designed to trap sand and restore the beach. Three additional breakwaters are planned to the north of the house. So far the breakwaters are working.

Four

THE LIFE-SAVING SERVICE AND SHIPWRECKS

The life-saving program in the United States came into being in 1871 under the able leadership of Mr. Sumner I. Kimball. Over the next few years, the success of the system led Congress to appropriate money to erect additional stations along the coast. The fledgling United States Life-Saving Service was determined to locate one of its many stations at the important entrance to the Chesapeake Bay. The entrances to bays and harbors presented special dangers to mariners, and a large number of maritime disasters occurred at those locations. Cape Henry was such a site, so a contract was awarded in 1874 to erect a life-saving station on the beach at Cape Henry. The building, from the plans for an 1874-type building, was constructed and operational in October of that year. The first keeper was appointed in December with an annual salary of $200. In January 1875, the first crew was discharged for insubordination, and they were replaced by an all-black crew.

In October 1906, the steamer *George Farwell*, its hold filled with lumber, approached Cape Henry in a thick fog. The ship went aground just south of the station, and a crew was dispatched to assist in a rescue. Using the Lyle gun, a line was established to the stricken vessel and 16 men were brought ashore in the breeches buoy. (Courtesy Old Coast Guard Station.)

The apparatus cart was used to bring the breeches buoy rescue apparatus down the beach to the shipwreck location in this 1912 image. The cart would be loaded and pulled to the rescue using the station crew or the station horse. The wooden wheels had a metal rims and were wide so they would not sink in the soft sand. (Courtesy Old Coast Guard Station.)

Here is a fully equipped Long Branch surfboat being loaded onto its wagon following a surfboat drill at the Cape Henry Life-Saving Station. Drills with the surfboat were conducted each Tuesday of the week. The men would try to launch the boat into the water within a minute and then they would practice rowing. (Courtesy Old Coast Guard Station.)

The station crew launches the 26-foot Long Branch surfboat during a crew drill. Launching the surfboat during storms was a dangerous task for the surfmen. Records give credit to the crews at Cape Henry for a number of rescues under rough conditions. The crew members became known as "storm warriors." (Courtesy Old Coast Guard Station.)

This 1911 photograph shows Keeper Nelson Holmes and the eight surfmen assigned to the Cape Henry Life-Saving Station. It was a noteworthy occasion when the entire crew would assemble for a photograph. The men signed on for one year and were initially paid $40 a month for each of the five months the station was operational (December through April). (Courtesy Old Coast Guard Station.)

Along the Virginia Beach coastline, the life-saving stations were from five to seven miles apart. As each watch started, the surfmen from Cape Henry would walk south along the beach toward the Virginia Beach station. At the halfway point, they would exchange checks and return to their own stations. This halfway house was located near present-day Sixty-Fourth Street. (Painting by Liz Tyler Mathis.)

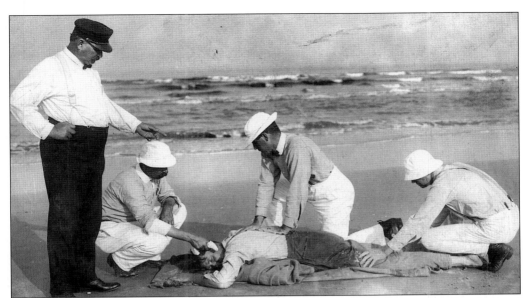

Cape Henry Life-Saving Station keeper Nelson Holmes instructs his crew in "methods of resuscitation." Daily drills were an integral part of the lifesavers' duties. Many of the drills were elaborately staged and photographed by the U.S. Life-Saving Service (USLSS) for government and private publications. Nelson Holmes was appointed keeper of the Cape Henry Station in 1898, when he was approximately 45 years old. (Courtesy Old Coast Guard Station.)

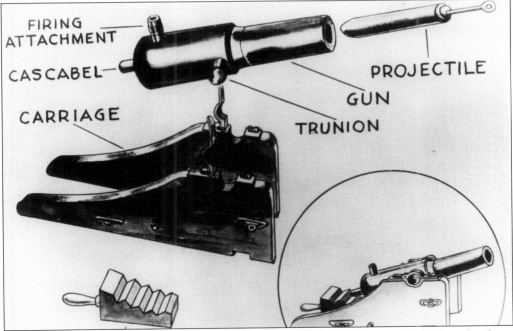

FIRING ATTACHMENT

CASCABEL

CARRIAGE

PROJECTILE

GUN

TRUNION

The Lyle gun was a line-throwing rescue apparatus used in conjunction with the breeches buoy or the life car. It was utilized to establish a secure line between the rescuers on the beach and the people on the stricken vessel. The breeches buoy was then hauled out to the vessel, and the survivor was brought ashore. (Courtesy Old Coast Guard Station.)

Keeper Nelson Holmes, his family, and some friends pose with the family cow in front of their house in 1900. Holmes married Annie Midgett, and together they had four sons and seven daughters during the period 1880 to 1900. Life certainly became a little easier when the railroad was extended to Cape Henry in 1902. (Courtesy Old Coast Guard Station.)

These are the two life-saving stations at Cape Henry. The structure on the left was the first-generation station built in 1874. The second-generation station was completed in 1904, and the old station was retained and used as a stable and a storehouse at times. Later a separate building was constructed to house the kitchen. (Courtesy Old Coast Guard Station.)

The second-generation life-saving station was constructed in 1904. It was an example of the Quonochontaug-type station, 21 of which were built along the East Coast. This sparsely detailed, one-and-a-half-story building featured a single gable roof pierced by a small dormer on each side and a large, hipped-roof tower at one end. The building was torn down in 1941. (Courtesy Old Coast Guard Station.)

The station crew at Cape Henry Coast Guard Station in 1929 posed in their dress uniforms. From left to right are Boatswain Charles O. Peel, Boatswain Mate (BM) 1st Class Daniel B. Ethridge, BM 1st Class Levy E. Newbern, and Surfmen Edwin Waterfield, Ralph Aydlett, Roy Lewark, Chester Robbins, Wilbur Snow, Richard A. Job, and B. Tillett. In August 1933, a large storm struck the Virginia coast at high tide and winds at Cape Henry were clocked at 82 miles per hour. (Courtesy the Mariner's Museum.)

The Coast Guard Station at Little Creek is shown here under construction. By 1938, the Cape Henry lifeboat station was in the line of fire of the coastal artillery batteries at Fort Story. A survey determined that a better facility should be constructed in the sheltered waters of Little Creek inside the Chesapeake Bay. Also the life-saving mission could be accomplished without over-the-beach operations. (Courtesy Old Coast Guard Station.)

The boathouse at the Little Creek Coast Guard Station was built in 1939. It housed the station surfboats with a launchway. The 1939 station building accomplished its mission until it was replaced with a more modern facility in 1996. At that time, the boathouse launchway was removed, but this facility was upgraded and is still in use today. The waters off Cape Henry are within the area of responsibility of the boats from this station.

Due to its location at the entrance to the safe harbors of Hampton Roads, Cape Henry was a magnet for shipwrecks. During the period from the establishment of the station until the USLSS became the U.S. Coast Guard in 1915, a total of over 50 wrecks occurred, none with loss of life. This shipwreck was on the beach in the vicinity of Eighty-Sixth Street. (Courtesy Kathryn Fisher.)

In 1906, the *Antonio* went aground in a gale and the lifesavers rescued the 11 crewmen without incident. The ship could not be saved. The crewmen, who had not been paid by the owner, got drunk and were removed into rooms in the old building. The ship's owner refused to pay the crew about $200, so the copper sheathing from the *Antonio*'s hull was sold and they were paid their due wages. (Courtesy Old Coast Guard Station.)

In January of 1937, the crew responded to the grounding of the *Annapolis* and two large barges that had grounded north of the station in a thick fog. Two lifeboats took up position on the beach and a Coast Guard cutter was on the scene. It took a week before salvage tugs could pull the *Annapolis* and the barges off the beach. (Courtesy Old Coast Guard Station.)

A violent hurricane in September 1944 caused a freighter to be stranded at Cape Henry. As the Cape Henry Coast Guard Station had been closed, the crew from Virginia Beach responded. A breeches buoy was set up, and the crew was brought safely to shore. The breeches buoy was later phased out as a rescue method and replaced with helicopters lowering rescue baskets. (Courtesy Old Coast Guard Station.)

As a result of severe erosion at Fort Story, any number of shipwreck remains can be uncovered. This section of Cape Henry is a favorite with beach walkers who find all kind of treasures, such as these remains of a wooden turn-of-the-century sailing vessel. This is probably a section of the keel showing the brass fasteners and wood treenails used to attach the ribbing to the frame.

Here is a piece of the stern of the Norwegian vessel *Dictator*, which was uncovered at the North End following Hurricane Grace in 1991. The Cape Henry crew assisted the Virginia Beach station in the 1891 rescue attempt. Five crewmen in addition to the captain's wife and son were lost. The events surrounding the tragic shipwreck resulted in the erection of the "Norwegian Lady" statue on the Virginia Beach boardwalk at Twenty-Fifth Street.

Following a storm in March 1989, these ship remains washed ashore at Fort Story. The hull section measured some 50 feet by 12 feet and is one of the largest pieces of shipwreck found in Virginia Beach. It was determined that it was the remains of the Italian bark *Francisco Bella Gamba*, which sank in 1878 en route from Genoa, Italy, to Baltimore. (Courtesy Old Coast Guard Station.)

None of those in Virginia Beach will ever forget Hurricane Isabel, which violently struck the East Coast in September 2003. A section of hull timbers measuring some 23 feet by eight feet was uncovered by the storm. It was found by Susan Werby while she was walking on the beach in October. Since the identification of the ship could not he determined, the shipwreck was designated as the *Susan W.* (Courtesy Bob Ruegsegger.)

The Old Coast Guard Station assembled a team to conduct research on the wreck of the *Susan W.* Joining the museum staff was Dr. John Broadwater (center) and his team from the NOAA Maritime Archaeology center at the Mariner's Museum in Newport News, Virginia. A thorough review was conducted, timbers measured, and the data compiled. (Courtesy Bob Ruegsegger.)

The 11th Transportation Battalion assisted in relocating the shipwreck from the surf. The exterior planking of the *Susan W* indicated a substantial vessel. It appears this was the hull of a cargo schooner from the second half of the 19th century. This type of vessel served as the interstate system of its day, moving cargo up and down the East Coast. The team was unable to determine the name of the vessel.

The Old Coast Guard Station Shipwreck Identification Project was initiated in 1996. It provides a method of documentation and research for pieces of shipwrecks that wash up on the beaches in Virginia Beach. This is the only such maritime project in Virginia. It this photograph, Museum Administrator Julie Pouliot and Director Fielding Tyler place an identification tag on the remains of the stern section of the *Francisco Bella Gamba.*

A plastic ID tag is nailed to a keel section of a wooden sailing vessel found on the beach at Cape Henry. The numbered tags match documentation maintained by the Old Coast Guard Station Museum. On some occasions, a shipwreck piece can be relocated, and some have been taken back out to sea. The museum gets a number of calls from beachcombers when a tagged piece resurfaces. (Photograph by Liz Tyler Mathis.)

Five

THE U.S. ARMY ARRIVES AND BUILDS A FORT

"We should put up a gigantic fortress right here between these capes," uttered Pres. William Howard Taft in November 1909 at Cape Henry. Taft, speaking to a convention of the Atlantic Deeper Waterways Association in Norfolk, had just consumed an enormous amount of Lynnhaven oysters, reputed to be as many as a barrel, at O'Keefe's Casino on the beach. He might have been referring to the middle of the bay entrance, but in any case a few years later, Fort Story was born. Such is the power of the Lynnhaven oyster! In March 1914, the Virginia General Assembly ceded 343 acres in six parcels to the federal government, and in late 1916, Virginia governor Henry Stuart broke ground on the fledgling fort and then attended an oyster roast. In February 1917, Lt. Col. Daniel Warren Ketcham, U.S. Military Academy (USMA) class of 1890, became the first post commander, and at the same time, two artillery companies arrived on post from Fort Monroe. Soldiers of the 10th Company, Coast Defenses of Chesapeake Bay, pose with their trophies in the photograph dated May 10, 1918. This company was a Virginia National Guard unit that replaced a regular army company, which had been deployed overseas. (Courtesy Garrison Commander, Fort Story.)

In July 1916, the War Department broke ground for a military reservation. The post was named for the former chief of artillery, Maj. Gen. John Patten Story, USMA 1865. Story was appointed to West Point in 1861 and graduated as a lieutenant of infantry. His first duty station was with the 16th Infantry in New York. He later served in the office of the chief signal officer in Washington, D.C. He was then assigned to West Point as an assistant professor of mathematics and later geography and history. After duty with an artillery battery, he returned for a second assignment with the signal service. As captain of the 4th Artillery, he served at Fort Warren, Massachusetts, and Fort Monroe, Virginia. In 1898, he was assigned to the Department of the East as an inspector. Story later served as the commanding officer at the Artillery School. He was promoted to brigadier general and transferred to Washington as chief of artillery. He was promoted to major general in that office and retired in 1905. He moved to California and continued to serve the army as a member of the Board of National Defense. After 40 years of service, John Patten Story died in 1915 in Pasadena, California.

In the image at right, Pvt. Joseph Napoleon Osborn is posing for a company photograph on April 25, 1918. Osborn was a member of the 2nd Company, Coast Artillery Corps, which had been transferred from Fort Monroe to Fort Story in February 1917. At this time, the company commander was Capt. Thomas Foster Witt, who also doubled as post commander for a short period. Witt was a graduate of the Virginia Military Institute, class of 1912. Two months after the arrival of the company, the United States declared war on Germany. The 2nd Company was assigned as the artillery crew for a pair of M1900 six-inch coast defense guns designated as Battery A. The guns had been dismounted from their platforms at Fort Monroe and moved forward to the cape. In 1921, the 2nd Company was transferred back to Fort Monroe and the guns were dismantled and placed in storage. The image below shows Osborn in the dress uniform of the Coast Artillery Corps. Osborn had served with General Pershing on the Mexican border at El Paso in 1916. (Courtesy Anne Osborn Cox.)

This is the concrete platform of one of the guns of Battery A as it appears today in the surf at Fort Story. The six-inch rapid-fire (RF) Model 1900 guns were complemented by a pair of five-inch RF Model 1897 guns, which were obsolete when they were mounted. Along with four five-inch rapid-fire guns on Fisherman Island at Cape Charles, this was the extent of the defense of the bay entrance.

This is a World War I recruiting poster for the Coast Artillery Corps. The Coast Artillery Corps largely served in fixed fortifications at the entrances of most of the continental harbors. Joining the coast artillery was not all stateside duty, as many units were sent to France to serve as heavy artillery. At this time, the Coast Artillery Corps also picked up the mission of antiaircraft artillery.

At Fort Monroe, the soldiers of the 2nd and 5th Coast Artillery companies lived in an 1879 two-story brick barracks on the parade ground inside the moat. The barracks had washrooms, kitchens, and steam heat. Then in the winter of 1917, the soldiers were pulled from their comfortable quarters and moved into tents at Cape Henry. The image depicts the tent city of the 2nd Company. (Courtesy Anne Osborn Cox.)

This photograph was taken from the new Cape Henry lighthouse and shows the barracks and other buildings constructed in 1917 and 1918 to house the Coast Artillery companies. When World War I ended, the soldiers returned to their home stations or were demobilized. The barracks were generally underutilized by the remaining caretaking detachment and deteriorated under the relentless winds common in the area.

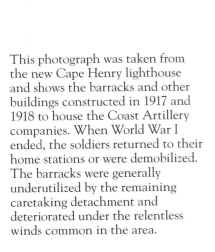

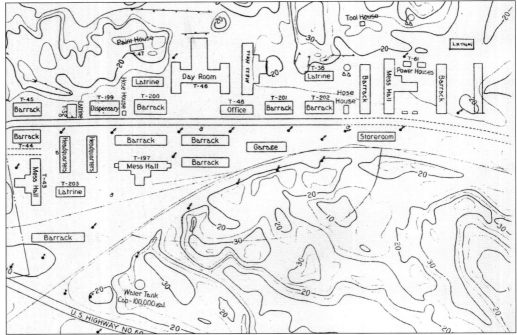

This map of the World War I 600-Series cantonment area was in use until a few years before the World War II. The buildings were then demolished and replaced with 700-Series buildings. There were accommodations for four artillery companies. Latrines were located in separate buildings. Building T-46 in the center of the image served as a day room for the garrison.

This is one of the four temporary mess halls used by the garrison. This mess served soldiers from a particular artillery company. For many years, the army maintained the structure of cooks and equipment managed at the company level. One of the mess halls at Fort Story was retained for various uses into the 1980s. At one point, it served as the Boy Scout hut for Troop 61.

First Lt. David Hottenstein, Coast Artillery Corps, served as commanding officer at Fort Story from June 1928 to June 1930. The troops stationed on post during this period were from Company D, 12th Coast Artillery Regiment, which had its headquarters at Fort Monroe. A majority of the commanders up until 1936 were lieutenants and only served for a few months.

The post headquarters building was constructed in 1918. It was built as a headquarters and has continuously served in that capacity. During the early 1930s, a few soldiers lived in the building, as the World War I barracks were drafty and cold. During World War II, an artillery observation platform was added on the roof.

This storehouse building near the headquarters structure is the only other building on post that dates to 1918. It has metal siding that was later replaced. After 87 years, the building is still standing and still functions as a warehouse. The 600 Series of World War I barracks and support building were classified as temporary, and nearly all were demolished by the late 1930s.

This is an interesting photograph taken by a soldier from the top of the new lighthouse in August 1937. In the right rear is the Cape Henry Coast Guard Station and some of the small cottages used by the surfmen and later occupied by soldiers with families. In the distance are the Hygeia Hotel and some large summer cottages. The World War I barracks are in the foreground.

This building was constructed in 1918 as the day room for the coast artillery garrison. When the support buildings were demolished, this was one of the few structures given a second life. For a period, it operated as the small commissary serving the military on post as well as the retired military living in the area. The commissary sold the cheapest cigarettes in Tidewater. It was closed down in 1974, and the building was demolished.

Albert Midgett's gas station and store was on the corner of 141st Street and Atlantic Avenue across from O'Keefe's Casino. Albert Midgett had retired from the lighthouse service and bought the property next to the Fort Story gate. At this time, there was no military fence, and access to the community went through the army installation. The army took over the property in 1939.

By 1921, Fort Story had a coastal defense mission but no armament except for three antiaircraft guns. In the summer of that year, the army started to build emplacements and powder and shell magazines for a battery of four M1920 16-inch howitzers mounted on M1920 barbette carriages. A lot of sand in the "desert" had to be moved around to accommodate the battery

A concrete tunnel was built under the secondary dune line in 1921 to allow access between the howitzer battery and the battery plotting room on the reverse slope. Rails were put inside the tunnel, allowing for overhead cover of the ammunition and shell carts. On occasion it was used to store the railway artillery of the 52nd Coast Artillery Regiment from Fort Eustis.

Pictured here is the east end of the 280-foot-long artillery tunnel under the secondary dune line. This photograph shows the 225-foot retaining wall leading to the gun batteries. The sand continued to drift, and at this entrance, from 12 to 15 cubic yards of sand had to be removed periodically. In 1933, the army planted vegetation on the dune line and stabilized the sand.

The concrete switchboard and plotting room was built on the reverse slope in 1922 to protect this vital facility from direct hostile fire. To the left of the plotting room was the post radio room. It was later upgraded to afford protection against a gas attack. Target acquisition was taken from soldiers in the observation towers on the beach and relayed to the plotting room.

This is Howitzer Number 4 of Battery Alexander C. M. Pennington in 1935. Pennington was a graduate of West Point who had served with distinction during the Civil War and retired in 1899 as a major general with more than 40 years of service. The soldier leaning on the barrel is F. Ray Shield of the Virginia National Guard in Onancock, Virginia. (Courtesy Frank Shield III.)

Steel-frame coast artillery observation towers were called "fire control" towers. This is the Granite C fire control tower built in 1940 on a tract of land acquired in 1914. Granite C provided fire control observations for Battery Pennington and two other artillery batteries. The name Granite was taken from the nearby sand pits of the Granite Brick Company. The towers are gone, and the Fort Story Club is at this location today.

In addition to coast artillery, the principal weapon used in fixed-location seacoast defense has been underwater mines. The minefield existed to destroy hostile vessels and close channels into a harbor. This "mining casemate" was built in 1922 to control some of the mines set out at the entrance to the Chesapeake Bay. It was activated in December 1941 and served an important role throughout World War II.

Here is a 155-mm GPF Model 1917 gun firing on the beach at Fort Story in 1936. When the guns were ready to fire, they were moved to the reinforced gun platforms commonly called "panama mounts." The panama mounts were built in three locations in 1931, 1933, and 1942. The 155-mm gun was not considered modern armament, and by 1944, they were no longer listed on the active status list. (Courtesy Casemate Museum.)

This photograph was taken in February 1936 from the top of the water tower at Fort Story. Snow is on the ground and the water along the beach is frozen. In the foreground of the picture are army mess halls, and on the lighthouse compound are the three original sets of quarters. (Courtesy Ed Amburn.)

The Hurricane of 1933 struck Virginia Beach and Cape Henry in August of that year with torrential rain and accompanying strong winds. The storm hit at high tide, breached the dunes, and swept over Atlantic Avenue. The Coast Guard station and the army barracks were heavily damaged. The roof was blown off Mr. Midgett's house, and this house, the summer cottage of Mr. Allen Willett, received heavy damage.

This 1941 photograph from the top of the old lighthouse shows the progress of military construction before World War II. The post theater is in the left foreground. The Army Quartermaster Corps was responsible for a massive program of building barracks, mess halls, chapels, and other buildings of the 700 Series at army posts all over the United States. Some are still in use today.

The 1st Battalion, 71st Coast Artillery, fires their three-inch guns at towed targets in this photograph dated January 1941. The battalion was conducting a demonstration for the commanding general of the First Army, Gen. Hugh A. Drum. Note the former Cape Henry Coast Guard Station at the end of the gun line. The weapons' firing was the reason that the station was moved inside the bay to Little Creek.

The eight-inch gun was mounted on railway carriages and included a battery train. In this photograph taken in the summer of 1938, Battery D, 246th Coast Artillery, Virginia National Guard, is conducting service practice. In early 1942, the eight-inch guns assigned to Battery Y at Fort Story were placed in caretaker status and the railway program was discontinued.

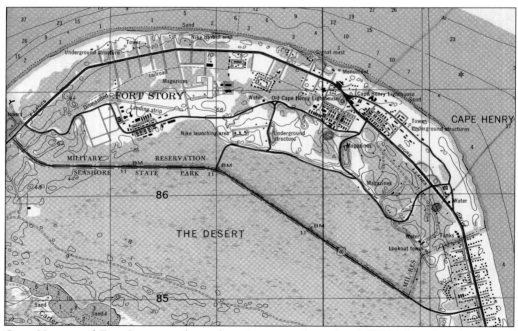

Cape Henry and Fort Story are shown here in a map sheet dated 1955. Note that the area of the state park is still referred to as the "desert." The residential community of the North End of Virginia Beach is on the right. In 1941, the army closed Route 60 (Shore Drive) through the post, and a new road was built through the State Park in a matter of months.

A number of the oceanfront cottages in the North End of Virginia Beach were built only for summer use. This substantial cottage was built in 1937 on an oceanfront lot bought by the Norfleet family for $2,500. It was the primary residence for the family and was three blocks from the east gate at Fort Story. The four Norfleet girls grew up here. (Courtesy Nancy Norfleet Carpenter.)

This log cabin was reportedly built at the turn of the 19th century, before the railroad was built and before Atlantic Avenue was paved. It was on the west side of Atlantic Avenue on what is now Seventy-Fourth Street in the North End. It was probably the only house in the area and was the summer residence of the Emmerson family of Portsmouth, Virginia, who had to ride in a beach buggy to get here.

When the army acquired the 343-acre parcel of land at Fort Story in 1917, it picked up small tracts along the oceanfront as future sites for artillery fire control towers. This was the "Emerson" site, named for the family who owned the nearby summer cottage. The first observation tower was built to support the 16-inch howitzer battery. A second tower was added to the site in 1941.

The houses at the North End of Virginia Beach come in all shapes and sizes. The community was at first largely comprised of summer cottages. Today a number of those cottages and rental houses have been replaced with full-time residences. This Spanish stucco house was built in 1925 on Eighty-Fifth Street. At one time, it was the residence of a retired captain who owned a parrot that the neighborhood kids loved to visit.

Pictured here are barracks of the Civilian Conservation Corps (CCC) in First Landing State Park. During the Great Depression, the federal government organized the CCC to give work to unemployed men. The first companies arrived in October 1933 and started a number of projects. Until 1940, the CCC companies built roads, trails, and cabins as well as support buildings. These former barracks are still in use at First Landing State Park.

This is one of the rental cabins in use at First Landing State Park. The men of the CCC built six cabins in addition to maintenance and administrative buildings. These cabins are still in use today. The CCC men were billeted in the park area but on some occasions occupied the World War II buildings on Fort Story.

When the soldiers of the 246th Coast Artillery Regiment were called to active duty in September 1940, the 700-Series barracks program was just beginning. With no permanent facilities available, the Virginia National Guard troops were billeted in this tent camp on the south end of the post adjacent to the east gate. By the end of 1941, all buildings were completed and in use.

In September 1940, the State Conservation Commission granted the War Department permission to use 700-plus acres of Seashore State Park to build a hospital and to expand its housing areas. This January 1941 aerial photograph shows barracks under construction for the 2nd Battalion, 71st Coast Artillery. In the background are the single-story buildings of the station hospital, which would be later be converted to a convalescent hospital

Six

DEFENDING THE CHESAPEAKE BAY

In the first days of December 1941, the Harbor Defenses of Chesapeake Bay were on partial alert and two batteries on full alert at Fort Story. The first report of the attack on Pearl Harbor was received at Fort Monroe by radio at 3:15 in the afternoon on December 7. At 4:00, the Harbor Defense Control Post and the alert batteries were directed to stand by. Two hours later, the entire harbor defense went on full alert, and throughout Tidewater, soldiers, sailors, and Marines were ordered back to their bases. The war had begun. Except for a weak underwater defense and the lack of armament protecting the northern approaches to the Chesapeake Bay, the Harbor Defenses of the Chesapeake Bay were prepared. The armament modernization program had barely gotten underway when the war started. The main armament of the outer line of the harbor defenses consisted of the minefield and the battery of 16-inch howitzers. Construction was beginning on the 16-inch primary and the 6-inch secondary weapons systems. This photograph depicts Gun Number 1 of Battery Alexander C. M. Pennington in 1948.

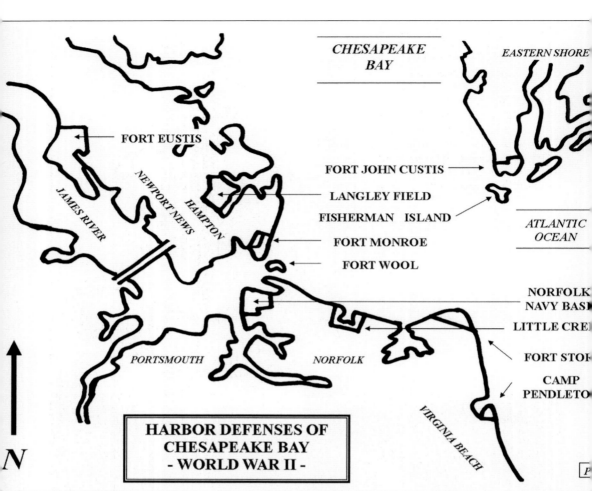

CHESAPEAKE BAY

EASTERN SHORE

FORT EUSTIS

JAMES RIVER

NEWPORT NEWS

HAMPTON

FORT JOHN CUSTIS

LANGLEY FIELD

FISHERMAN ISLAND

FORT MONROE

FORT WOOL

ATLANTIC OCEAN

NORFOLK NAVY BASE

LITTLE CREEK

FORT STORY

CAMP PENDLETON

PORTSMOUTH

NORFOLK

VIRGINIA BEACH

N

**HARBOR DEFENSES OF
CHESAPEAKE BAY
- WORLD WAR II -**

Prior to World War I, most of the armament of the Harbor Defenses of Chesapeake Bay (HDCB) was situated at Fort Monroe, far back from the entrance to the bay. The 16-inch howitzers at Fort Story did not have the range to close the entrance. In 1940, Brig. Gen. Rolin L. Tilton assumed command of the HDCB, and formal approval was given to add 6- and 16-inch batteries on Cape Henry and Cape Charles. A 6-inch battery was approved for Fort Wool. When the final defenses were in place, the outer defenses between Cape Charles and Cape Henry were anchored by a minefield. At Cape Charles, guns were emplaced at Fort John Custis and on Fisherman Island. On the southern flank, Fort Story and the Little Creek Mine Command provided the defenses. The inner defenses were anchored at Fort Monroe and Fort Wool. For the duration of the conflict, the soldiers of the harbor defenses stayed with their guns. Following that, the organization was drawn down and the armament was dismantled.

This is the coat of arms of the Harbor Defenses of Chesapeake Bay (HDCB). The Cape Henry cross is depicted in the center. Under the leadership of Brigadier General Tilton, the command performed its defensive mission in an outstanding manner. In 1946, Tilton was relieved of command. The following year, the armament was scrapped and the HDCB had successfully completed its mission.

Gun Number 1, Battery Alexander C. M. Pennington, was manned by Battery B, 246th Coast Artillery, Virginia National Guard, during a service practice in 1941. Battery B served in the Civil War as the Danville Grays and served with distinction at First Manassas and Gettysburg. It also served as an infantry company in France during World War I. This image is taken from a short film clip.

Projectiles and powder were loaded into the breech of an M1920 16-inch howitzer during service practice in 1941. Each of the four howitzers was mounted on a circular concrete gun platform, enabling the weapons to be fired in any direction. Initially cover from plunging overhead hostile fire was not provided. A narrow-gauge railroad system allowed the ammunition to be moved rapidly between the magazines and the gun positions.

The blue denim–clad gun crew from Battery A, 246th Coast Artillery, poses with a 16-inch howitzer in June 1941 during service practice. This battery was originally from Lynchburg and had seen World War I duty in France with the 42nd Infantry Division. The battery is still serving today as the 1st Battalion, 246th Field Artillery of the 29th Infantry Division (Light), Virginia Army National Guard.

The 155-mm GPF gun was intended for mobile defenses within the harbor defenses. In September 1940, the 244th Coast Artillery Regiment, New York National Guard, was called to active duty at the Virginia State Rifle Range, later renamed Camp Pendleton. This photograph was taken on January 10, 1941, during an inspection of the harbor defenses by the commanding general of the First Army, Lt. Gen. Hugh A. Drum.

This November 1945 photograph shows one of the two entrances to the command post of the Harbor Defenses of Chesapeake Bay. It was located on the reverse slope of the secondary dune line as protection from hostile fire. The reinforced concrete building was 150 feet in length and was completed in the summer of 1943 at a cost of $100,000. Following hostilities, the building was used for a time by army transportation units.

In September 1940, final approval was given by the secretary of war for the harbor defense modernization program, which included two batteries of 16-inch guns at Fort Story. The modern batteries were designed to have all components provided with massive overhead cover as protection from threats from the surface as well as the air. This is Battery Construction Number 120, which was started in April 1941 on the high ground along the secondary dune line in the "desert." It offered excellent fields of fire for the pair of navy Mark II, M1 guns. A separate plotting room was built some 200 yards away on the reverse slope of the dune line. In November 1943, the battery was finally completed and named in honor of Brig. Gen. Daniel W. Ketcham, USMA 1890. The soldiers of Battery C, 246th Coast Artillery were assigned to the most modern weapons system in the harbor defenses. With the reduction in the threat to our shores, Battery Ketcham and other batteries were reduced from alert status in 1944. It had never fired a shot in anger.

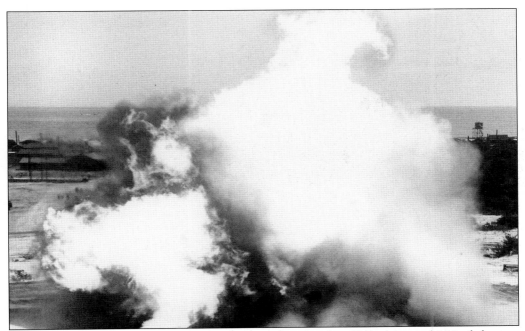

A proof firing for Battery Ketcham was conducted in October 1942. A second 16-inch battery was under construction in 1942 but would not be ready for proof firing until February 1945. With the victory in Europe in May 1945, the alert status of the harbor defenses was further reduced. There was an uncertainty as to the immediate future of the entire defensive system.

The Coast Artillery Corps tested a remote control watercraft off Cape Henry in May 1941. In this photograph, M.Sgt. John Lucas on the Army Mine Planter *Schofield* is operating a "radio impulse machine" to control movement of a crewless test boat. The crewless vessel would be used to tow offshore targets for gunnery practice of the anti–motor torpedo boat batteries at Fort Story.

In 1942, construction was started on a new 90-mm M1 gun battery on the beach. The battery was a self-contained emplacement, with the plotting room and shell rooms in a single structure. The pair of 90-mm guns was for use in anti–motor torpedo boat role and also to cover the mine field at the entrance to the bay. This photograph was taken when the battery was completed in 1943.

The Aircraft Warning Service was activated in 1942 with the mission of providing enemy aircraft observation posts for the U.S. Army Air Force. This observation post was located on the beach at what was then 118th Street at the North End. The volunteers at that post consisted of men and women who lived in the area. This structure and sign have recently been discovered on private property.

This 1942 photograph shows one of two modern six-inch batteries under construction on the south end of the post. Battery Cramer was designed as a secondary harbor defense weapon complementing the 16-inch guns. The sand-covered reinforced concrete structure contained a number of powder and shell rooms in addition to a plotting room. Other rooms were built to house the power generators, communications, and storage space. The two M1903 six-inch guns were manufactured at the Watervliet Arsenal in New York and shipped by rail to Fort Story. The gun crews were protected from small arms fire by cast-iron shields. Battery Cramer remained in active status until July 1945, and the guns were removed in 1949 and sold for scrap. The casemate structure served the army and navy for other uses for many years afterward. To cover the entrance to the Chesapeake Bay, similar six-inch batteries were built on Fisherman Island and at Fort John Custis on the tip of the Eastern Shore of Virginia.

The gun crew of a three-inch antiaircraft gun and their mascot are pictured here at Fort Story in 1941. The 71st Coast Artillery was a new antiaircraft unit that moved to Fort Story in 1940. Basic training was conducted on post, and the draftees initially lived in the vintage World War I barracks. The "Rollin' Seventy First" departed Fort Story, saw service in Europe, and later served as a missile battalion during the cold war.

The artillery batteries at Fort Story used observation towers on the coast to locate and position targets offshore. The data used a method of triangulation to locate a target for the artillery. Information was then relayed to the firing battery. This steel-frame tower was built in 1925 at the State Rifle Range south of the town of Virginia Beach, and it was used to support the 16-inch howitzer batteries.

When the land that would become Fort Story was ceded to the federal government in 1914, five additional parcels of land along the beachfront were also acquired. These were designated for use as future locations for artillery fire control towers. It would be more than 25 years before this property located between 105th and 106th Streets would be used. Parcel C was located south of the post on the beach in an area that had been platted by the Cape Henry Syndicate. The army erected two steel-frame towers with three observation rooms on each tower. Each observation room supported a designated artillery battery. With the drawdown at the end of World War II, the towers were declared surplus and closed. The U.S. Navy took over the site after the departure of the coast artillery soldiers. In 1960, Tower B, depicted in this 1948 photograph, was demolished. Tower A was taken over by the navy and later used by the Naval Surface Warfare Center. When that technology was no longer needed, it was demolished in 2003.

In this photograph, taken in the summer of 1944, the khaki-clad soldiers of Battery H, 2nd Coast Artillery pose in front of Battery 21. The 2nd Coast Artillery was a regular army regiment constituted in 1798, with its headquarters at Fort Monroe. A few months after this photograph was taken, Battery H was re-designated as Battery E. By the summer of 1945, only Battery E and Battery Cramer, with their fire control towers and supporting searchlights, remained on alert status. At that time, 1st Lt. Harold Heischober, former city councilman and vice mayor of Virginia Beach, commanded Battery E at this position. After the war, the 90-mm guns were removed and the building served a variety of army and navy missions, including the post Military Police Station. It is presently in use by the 396th Transportation Detachment (Harbormaster). The harbormaster detachment provides operational control for vessel and harbormaster operations. (Courtesy Garrison Commander, Fort Story.)

The Examination Battery (Battery 19) was located on the western perimeter of the installation adjacent to Seashore State Park (now First Landing State Park). It was built on Parcel E, one of the five parcels of property acquired by the army in 1914. An examination vessel was one of the first measures instituted for the protection of Hampton Roads ports. The examination vessel was responsible for the examination of all merchant vessels and small craft entering or departing the Virginia capes. This shore battery came online in the summer of 1942 and was in support of that vessel. The battery mounted two M1902 rapid-fire guns that were relocated forward from Battery Lee on Fort Wool. In addition to this battery, there were three artillery fire control towers and a switchboard building on the parcel titled "Granite." This June 1942 photograph was taken from one of those towers. Only the battery magazine remains. The Fort Story Club is presently adjacent to this site.

In February 1943, construction commenced on a two-gun battery of the new 90-mm guns. Battery Number 22 consisted of two 90-mm M1, fixed-mount, anti–motor torpedo boat guns mounted on these concrete gun blocks. Following the war, the battery was dismantled, and the wooden support buildings were demolished. Over the years, erosion crept in, and by 2001, the guns blocks had collapsed from their own weight.

The Medical Detachment, 246th Coast Artillery Regiment, is shown at the Fort Story obstacle course in this 1941 photograph. The 246th Coast Artillery was a Virginia National Guard unit and was called to active duty at Fort Story in September 1940. The Medical Detachment was activated from their station in Roanoke. Maj. H. H. Hurt served as a surgeon at the station hospital and lived with his family on 101st Street in Virginia Beach.

Depicted is the "600 Area" taken from the old Cape Henry lighthouse in 1950. In 1940, a massive construction program of barracks, mess halls, administration, and other buildings was initiated by the Quartermaster Corps. The primary emphasis was on speed of construction to get the soldiers out of the tents. These barracks were initially occupied by coast artillery soldiers, who were replaced by men from the assigned transportation companies. They remained in use until the late 1980s, when they were demolished. The standard 63-man, two-story barracks buildings had drop siding and were classified as temporary. During World War II, all buildings at Fort Story were painted in a camouflage pattern. The barracks were built in a company group with three barracks, a mess hall, and a supply/administration building. The barracks interiors were unfinished with open squad bays, NCO rooms, gang showers, and an indoor latrine with urinal troughs. They were heated by a coal-fired, central hot-air furnace. The Virginia Army National Guard maintains one barracks in the original configuration at the State Military Reservation.

On the night of June 12, 1942, the German submarine U-701 surfaced off the coast of Virginia Beach. She had departed the French port of Brest nearly a month earlier with the mission of planting underwater mines at the entrance to the Chesapeake Bay. The U-701 carried 15 mines to be dropped in the ship channel directly off Cape Henry. As the submarine came closer to shore, the lookout saw the lights of the town and automobile headlights. The U-701 then turned to starboard and cruised on the surface along the North End beaches headed toward Cape Henry. The lookouts guided the bow on the flickering Cape Charles lighthouse. As the Cape Henry lighthouse came up on the port side, the order was given to launch the mines from the torpedo tubes. Despite spotting a trawler in the channel, the mining was complete with the timing devices set to activate in 60 hours, giving plenty of time for the U-701 to be far out of the area.

On the afternoon of June 15, 1942, the American tanker *Robert C. Tuttle* shook as if it had hit something and then a column of smoke erupted from the ship. Four miles off the Virginia Beach boardwalk, the first mine had completed its work on a small convoy in single file preparing to enter the Chesapeake Bay. An artillery observer in one of the fire control towers reported the explosion, and the gun batteries went on alert. A second explosion occurred 30 minutes later as a mine detonated under the tanker *Esso Augusta*. The engines shut down and her rudder was blown off. Everyone was convinced that there was an enemy submarine in the area. A few days later, it was determined that enemy mines were responsible and minesweepers were called in from Yorktown. A large crowd of onlookers gathered on the boardwalk in Virginia Beach as the war came to America.

The mines continued to take their toll. To the south, the British trawler *Kingston Ceylonite* was escorting the last ship in the convoy. Believing that the convoy was under attack, the trawler raced north and other vessels signaled her to look out for mines. The *Ceylonite* did not have time to respond before she was blown out of the water. She went down with a loss of two officers and 18 men.

In March 1942, the first German U-boat scored a kill off Cape Henry. The SS *Tiger* was inbound from Aruba with navy fuel oil on board. Just off Cape Henry, she stopped to pick up a harbor pilot at night. She was struck by a torpedo from the U-754; the explosion ruptured a bulkhead, and the ship was plunged into darkness. She was later taken under tow but eventually sank.

Pictured here are Maj. and Mrs. Montroville B. Walker Jr. with their family in 1945. Maj. Walker had served in the office of the post engineer at Camp Pendleton and was transferred during the war to Fort Story as the post engineer. The family rented the "log cabin" on 118th Street for 10 years. It had been built in the late 1920s as a summer home for Mr. and Mrs. Harry C. Link.

In April 1941, the army closed the portion of Route 60 through the post. A bypass was debated by state highway officials, nature lovers, and local residents. Despite the protests, the War Department approved the project. Contractors bulldozed trees and completed a two-lane road through the cypress swamp adjacent to the fence line. This lower gate provided access to the new road, providing a third entrance to the post.

This is the 1945 Thanksgiving dinner menu for the Fort Story Provisional Battalion. By this time, the last remaining coast artillery soldiers at Fort Story were organized into a provisional battalion with three firing batteries under the Harbor Defenses of Chesapeake Bay. This menu served up everything from roast turkey to pumpkin pie to coffee and cigars. The war had ended, but the last of the 16-inch gun batteries was just being completed. Shortly after Thanksgiving, Battery D, Provisional Battalion, conducted the first practice on the new guns, firing 20 of the 2,000-pound rounds out to sea. They recorded two hits. In the following summer, Battery D fired another service practice with the 16-inch guns. When the guns were scheduled to fire a service practice, a notice was sent to local residents so they could remove their plates from the walls and make other preparations to avoid damage.

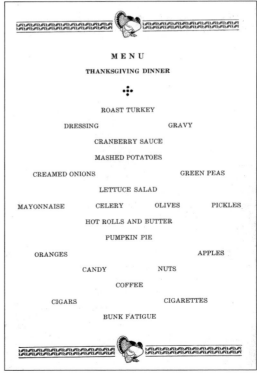

MENU

THANKSGIVING DINNER

ROAST TURKEY

DRESSING   GRAVY

CRANBERRY SAUCE

MASHED POTATOES

CREAMED ONIONS   GREEN PEAS

LETTUCE SALAD

MAYONNAISE   CELERY   OLIVES   PICKLES

HOT ROLLS AND BUTTER

PUMPKIN PIE

ORANGES   APPLES

CANDY   NUTS

COFFEE

CIGARS   CIGARETTES

BUNK FATIGUE

In addition to the main guns, each battery was provided with .50-caliber machine guns and 37-mm guns for close-in protection. Trenches were dug along the dunes to provide observation on the beachfront. Although the primary artillery was declared surplus in 1949, the soldiers of the Harbor Defenses of Chesapeake Bay practiced firing at towed aerial targets in front of Battery Cramer.

It was not all work for the soldiers assigned to man the big guns. The resort community of Virginia Beach was just a few miles to the south and provided a wide variety of entertainment, especially in the summer. Grumpy's offered beer, sodas, ice cream, and sandwiches to tourists and the soldiers from Camp Pendleton and Fort Story.

In 1940, the War Department acquired over 700 acres of property from the Commonwealth of Virginia to expand the post. That expansion included land to construct a station hospital on the western end of the post. It was originally decided to build it on the waterfront, but that decision was reversed. In 1941, the hospital was completed and occupied by the 160th Station Hospital. The single-story facility used theater-of-operations–type construction, which was temporary in nature. The hospital served the assigned soldiers throughout the war. In 1944, convalescent hospitals were authorized to prepare ambulatory patients for return to duty. Fort Story was selected because of its geographical location. It was also selected because the reduction in troop population with the departure of the coast artillery soldiers had left ample facilities. Programs included general education, vocational counseling, occupational therapy, recreation, athletics, and entertainment. There were stables offering horseback riding, and swimming was popular with the patients. Italian POWs performed menial tasks for the hospital staff. The Red Cross Gray Ladies acted as hostesses in the recreational building. The hospital closed in 1946, and all of the structures were immediately demolished.

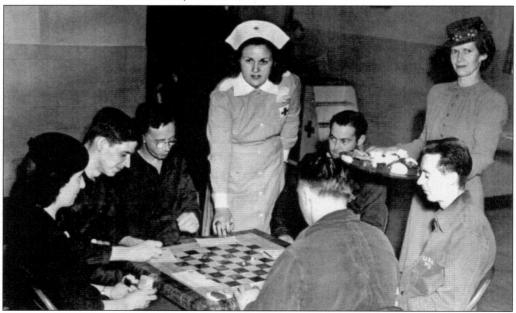

Throughout the war, an outer minefield extended across the mouth of the Chesapeake Bay from Cape Henry to Cape Charles. To operate the fields, mine casemates were located at Fort Story and on Fisherman Island on the Eastern Shore. The Mine Command for the Harbor Defenses of Chesapeake Bay was located at the Little Creek Mine Base inside the lower bay. The command laid the fields and supported the mine-laying operations with boats.

By 1929, latrines were built for the soldiers serving the 16-inch howitzer batteries. There were separate rooms for the officers and the enlisted men. With the advent of World War II, all of the buildings were painted with a three-color camouflage pattern. To provide additional camouflage, the army planted fast-growing kudzu vines on the gun positions. It worked, but the kudzu is still growing today.

On the oceanfront at Seventy-Seventh Street at the North End of Virginia Beach stands the stately Cooke-Royster Cottage. Today, nearly 90 years since it was first built, it still looms large and sturdy among its more modern neighbors. In 1916, Mr. F. S. Royster wanted a summer home for his children and grandchildren with enough room for all of the family at the same time. The cottage was complete in the summer of 1917 and was one of the very few houses in the area. At that time, there was no paved road to the cottage and the family would travel to and from Norfolk by rail or on the trolley. The house had three floors with large porches on three sides. There were six bedrooms on the second floor and two large rooms on the third floor. The ground floor had an expansive living room, a family dining room, and a children's dining room. Today the refurbished cottage stands with only a few modern changes.

In 1925, the army built a steel range tower on the secondary dune line in an area referred to locally as "the Hollies." It was intended to provide observation and fire control for the recently emplaced howitzers of Battery Pennington. In 1942, an additional tower was built on the Hollies tract, followed by two searchlight platforms at the base of the hill. This 1948 photograph shows the 1925 tower being dismantled.

The welder's torch has just brought down the last of the "Emerson" fire control towers in 1949. The towers were originally located between 109th and 111th Street adjacent to the Holly Road right-of-way. Prior to the army selling the property, the high ground served as a parking spot for local couples with a wonderful view of the moon rising over the ocean. Homes now occupy the site once known as "Pirate's Hill."

This is Gun Number 1, assigned to Battery Cramer. In July 1948, Battery Cramer fired its last service practice, and by 1949, the modern six-inch guns were declared surplus, along with the assigned artillery fire control towers and searchlights. This photograph was taken in 1949, when the gun was about to be scrapped. The crane at the right is ready to remove the gun barrel.

By 1948, the concept of harbor defense by long-range artillery was abandoned and the orders came down to scrap the guns. The scrapping of the 16-inch howitzers and guns took many months. First the ammunition had to be removed, and the barrel and the carriage were cut up. The Coast Artillery Corps was then abolished as a separate branch of the U.S. Army. (Photograph by Fielding Tyler.)

Seven

THE ARMY AMPHIBIANS
CHANGE THE MISSION

The DUKW amphibious vehicle served the U.S. Army during World War II, transporting men and equipment over the beaches of Normandy and other landings. More than 37,000 of these amphibious workhorse vehicles were built during World War II. Commonly called the "Duck," the vehicle was built on a two-and-a-half-ton truck chassis and moved on land and water with no special preparations. It was the truck that swims. In the summer of 1948, major elements on post included the 54th Transportation Truck Battalion with assigned DUKW companies. Later the 4th and 5th Transportation Commands took over operations on the post. The family of amphibious vehicles changed over time, with the workhorse DUKW being phased out in favor of more modern LARC (Lighter, Amphibious, Resupply, Cargo) vehicles. The Logistics-Over-the-Shore (LOTS) series of exercises tested the ability of the Transportation Corps to provide ship-to-shore and inland movement of supplies and equipment. Units from Fort Story continued to deploy overseas in support of worldwide transportation requirements.

The 425th Amphibious Truck Company was activated at Fort Story in July 1946 and was issued the DUKW vehicle. It was the first DUKW unit on post. The 425th had seen service as a DUKW company at Normandy and into France and Central Europe. The company later converted to the LARC V and in 1966 deployed to Vietnam and was assigned to river patrol boats.

In 1962, a strong storm struck the coast of Virginia and North Carolina. Named the "Ash Wednesday Storm," it caused widespread damage along the coast, including Virginia Beach. The tides and rain caused Atlantic Avenue to flood, and the residents were unable to evacuate. The 10th Transportation Battalion provided DUKW vehicles to transport the residents to shelters and other destinations.

Here is a line of LARC V amphibious vehicles from the 458th Transportation Company, 79th Transportation Battalion, off Red and Blue beaches. The vehicles are preparing to enter the U.S. Army vessel *John U. D. Page* during wedlock training off Cape Henry in August 1975. The LARC was the next generation of vehicles to replace the DUKW.

The LARC XV has a 15-ton cargo capacity and carries a greater payload than its cousin, the LARC V. It was capable of moving cargo from an offshore vessel to an inland location. The LARC XV made its mark in South Vietnam, where it operated in unimproved port areas.

These are cabins that belonged to 4-H Camp Farrar, established in 1948 at the end of Eighty-Fifth Street in what was then Seashore State Park. During the summer, campers would enjoy the beaches at the North End. These cabins were former World War II POW cabins that had been relocated to Camp Farrar. The camp and the adjacent Baptist Lodge on Eighty-Fourth Street were later closed, and the land reverted to the State Park.

Many of the houses in the North End were constructed during the building boom in Tidewater following World War II. There were some permanent residents, but they were largely summer and rental cottages. Also in 1947, the streets were renumbered from three digits to two starting at Sixty-Second Street. For example, 118th Street was renumbered Eighty-First Street. In 1980, Fort Story also renamed their numbered streets for amphibious operations.

The army actually first conducted LOTS operations at Vera Cruz during the Mexican War in 1847, using specially designed landing barges. This is an aerial view of an offload exercise during JLOTS II in September and October 1984. At that time, it was the largest joint exercise ever held on these beaches. More than 3,000 military personnel from the navy, active army, and army reserve components participated.

This is the second-generation family of amphibious vehicles that replaced the aging DUKW, which was phased out of the army inventory. From left to right are the LARC LX, the LARC XV, and the LARC V. The amphibians were the principal craft used to transfer cargo from vessels offshore to shore unloading points. Despite these new vehicles and a new nomenclature, the local civilian community continued to refer to all amphibious vehicles as "Ducks."

Amphibious vehicles are shown unloading cargo on Red and Blue beaches during an exercise in August 1975. The army landing craft and forklift are essential pieces of equipment in the logistics equation. This has been a familiar scene on all of the beaches, as units from Fort Eustis and Fort Story as well as transportation units from the reserve components utilize the beaches and inland training areas.

The first LARC LX amphibious vehicles came to Fort Story in 1954. At first it was designated as the Barge, Amphibious, Resupply, Cargo (BARC), later re-designated as the Lighter, Amphibious, Resupply, Cargo (LARC LX). It was the largest of the army amphibians ever developed and had a 60-ton payload capacity. The versatile LARC LX served at Fort Story until 2001, when it was phased out of the inventory and the 309th Transportation Detachment was inactivated.

The Lighter, Amphibian, Air Cushion Vehicle (LACV-30) was the third generation of amphibious vehicles replacing the LARC family. It was designed to ride on a four-foot cushion of air over the water and over land. The first vehicles began training at Fort Story in 1983 and could accommodate a 30-ton payload with speeds of more than 50 miles per hour. They were a part of the heavy-lift LOTS program. A completely new, modern facility, including a flyway to the water, was built on the western end of the post to accommodate these air-cushion vehicles, but the use of the air-cushion vehicle as a factor in amphibious logistics came to an end in 1994. The LACV was a noisy and maintenance-intensive vehicle, and the army determined to retire the hovercraft from the inventory. Accordingly, the 8th and 331st Transportation Companies were inactivated. The era of the amphibious vehicles, started at Cape Henry in 1946, had come to an end. To fill the space, the 7th Transportation Group relocated troops from Fort Eustis.

In 1950, the Army Antiaircraft Command activated 90- and 120-mm gun battalions that were later converted to missile batteries. By 1957, a gun battery relocated from Norfolk and became a Nike Ajax missile unit at Fort Story. In 1958, the battery received the Nike Hercules missile. The Nike missiles were to counter the Soviet bomber threat and were deployed at sites in a circular pattern around American industrial and military locations.

A typical Nike missile battery was divided into three major areas located on three separate parcels of land. The Integrated Fire Control (IFC) site contained the radar and radar equipment for acquiring and tracking the target and the missile. Battery B, 4th Battalion, 1st Artillery, operated this IFC site until they were inactivated in 1974. The buildings on this site are still used by the U.S. Marine Corps Recon School.

The Nike missile launch facility at Fort Story had three underground magazines. The missiles were stored and maintained underground. In an alert status, they were brought to the surface and raised to an 85-degree angle for firing. Other launch area facilities consisted of buildings for assembly of the warheads, liquid fuel area, power generation, and a ready room for the soldiers. The adjacent former 16-inch coast artillery battery also served as a field maintenance shop.

The administration area for the battery contained the barracks, mess hall, recreational facilities, and administrative offices. This facility was within walking distance of the launch facility. The missiles at the Nike sites were never fired. The crews were sent to Fort Bliss, Texas, for live firing on a range. These buildings have been consistently used by the army since its missile mission ceased in 1974.

This wooden building served as the post fire department for over 50 years, from 1941 until it was torn down in 1994. Fire in the hundreds of World War II wooden structures with coal-burning stoves was a constant danger. The platoon sergeant would remind his men that the barracks would "burn down in less than a minute." In 1994, an Emergency Services Center was built to house the fire department and the provost marshall's office.

This building was constructed during World War II on the former Granite tract on the west end of the post. In July 1946, an addition was constructed by German POWs from the confinement facility at Camp Ashby. Over the years, the club was well used by the military and retired communities. It was renovated in 1993 and is now the Fort Story Club. Both of the author's daughters had their wedding receptions at the club.

On a stormy night in October 1906, the steamer *George Farwell* ran aground just south of the Cape Henry Life-Saving Station. The conditions were far from ideal, and it took the surfmen 24 hours to complete the rescue of the 16-man crew. Most of the cargo of lumber was salvaged, but the vessel was declared a total loss and left on the beach. When the army established Fort Story in 1914, the boundary between the post and Princess Anne County ended at the water on the spot where the remains of the *George Farwell* rested. Over the years, the vessel broke up until only the boiler of the steamship remained. In this 1952 photograph, Peggy Norfleet sits on top of what all locals referred to as "the wreck" or "the boiler." For over 75 years, it was a landmark destination for the residents of the North End. In 1982, the top portion of the turbine was removed and relocated to the grounds of the Old Coast Guard Station. The actual boiler is still under the sand. (Courtesy Nancy Norfleet Carpenter.)

Balloons have a long history of service in military operations. During World War I, U.S. balloon observers trained at the Lee Hall Balloon School on the Virginia peninsula. In 1995–1996, the army and navy tested the use of balloons to transfer cargo from container ships offshore to the beach. The tests at Fort Story used winches and cables to transfer cargo under the balloon. This system never made it past the test stage.

The army closed down the coast defense system in Hampton Roads in 1950. But in 1976, it was discovered that all of the armament had not been removed. A pair of 90-mm gun mounts was still in position on the remote Fisherman Island off Cape Charles. The 7th Transportation Group from Fort Eustis sling-loaded the guns, and a CH-54 Flying Crane helicopter brought them to Fort Monroe.

The transportation companies at Fort Eustis and Fort Story conducted training in terminal service operations, loading and unloading cargo from vessels offshore or in ports. If the vessels were not available then training aids were used. The 438th Transportation Company built this mockup to train in offloading cargo. It was located in the former hospital area and was dubbed the *Neversail II*.

This east gate at Fort Story was rebuilt before World War II and remained in generally the same configuration until 2004. At that time, it was reconfigured as a result of the transition from an "open post" to one with access control and greater force protection. Modifications in 2004 included a new visitor center as well as both car and truck inspection lanes with an overhead canopy and lighting.

Over the years, the army has built fences on the beach to deter unauthorized walkers. During World War II, a wood and wire fence was built around the perimeter with a wooden path for guards. They fell apart after the conflict and were replaced with chain link fence. In this postwar image, it appears that concertina wire was the barrier of choice. The fences never deterred the beach strollers. (Courtesy Kathryn Fisher.)

The last of the army amphibians is on display near the lighthouses. The army amphibian force roamed the beaches at Cape Henry for some 50 years before being retired. After its use by the army, this LARC was used by the Virginia Beach Fire Department. For a number of years, it participated in the annual ceremonies of the commemoration of the wreck of the *Dictator* at the Norwegian Lady Park on Twenty-Fifth Street.

Eight

INTO THE 21ST CENTURY

SEALs from Naval Special Warfare Group 2 use the beaches and waters off Cape Henry for realistic training. Navy SEALs (Sea, Air, and Land) take their name from the elements in and from which they operate. The communities of Cape Henry and Fort Story are moving rapidly into the 21st century. The Virginia Department of Conservation and Recreation will continue to provide a natural legacy of outdoor activities and programs and at First Landing State Park. These efforts ensure that the best of Virginia's natural resources will be protected and available for future generations. The Lynnhaven River 2007 initiative has the goal of a clean and healthy Lynnhaven River and a plan to seed the river with oysters. The Department of Defense activities at Fort Story will remain and continue to be stewards of their land and waters off Cape Henry. The addition of the Special Operations training at Fort Story will effectively utilize the available training areas and complement the transportation LOTS and port operations missions. The civilian communities on both sides of the installation continue to grow and work in harmony with the military presence on post. The communities are ready to step up their role in the commemoration of Virginia Beach 2007 in recognition of the 400th anniversary of the first landing at Cape Henry in April 2007.

The entrance to the Chesapeake Bay at Cape Henry provides realistic and challenging training conditions across a broad spectrum of vital joint conventional and unconventional war-fighting skills. As the army's primary Joint Logistics-Over-The-Shore (JLOTS) training site, Cape Henry offers variable tides and currents in both the bay and the ocean. It also offers broad beaches, dunes, and coastal inland areas for training for all of the military services. Over 50,000 personnel are trained annually at Fort Story, and most are from units not stationed at Fort Story. The 2005 base closing and realignment proposal retains Fort Story but will shift operational command to the U.S. Navy. Future facilities include a close-quarters combat trainer and a multipurpose weapons training range. The quality of life for Fort Story families continues to be upgraded with the renovation and construction of new modern family housing units. (Courtesy Public Affairs Office, Fort Story.)

This northward view of the meeting of the Atlantic Ocean and the Chesapeake Bay is one of the most picturesque at Cape Henry. The wooden ramp leads from the Battle of the Capes monuments below. This area is a feeding area for porpoise, and they can be seen from this overlook. Also the visitor can see both naval and commercial traffic traversing to and from the ports of Hampton Roads.

The remains of 64 Chesapeake Indians were relocated to the sandy woods of the First Landing State Park in the spring of 1997. Among the features to be added to the park is a Chesapeake/Nansemond lineal village that will tell the story of these two tribes in Southeastern Virginia. (Courtesy Tony Belcastro.)

First Landing State Park maintains stewardship of 2,880 acres at Cape Henry. Nearly 1.8 million visitors annually use overnight accommodations, cabins, campsites, and day-use facilities with access to the beach on the Chesapeake Bay. In this building, the park maintains an information center in cooperation with the City of Virginia Beach and a Bay Lab with the Virginia Aquarium and Marine Science Center.

Here is the trail center at First Landing State Park. The park has 19 miles of hiking trails, with the Cape Henry trail offering multipurpose biking and hiking activities. The park also offers a boat launch ramp at the Narrows landing on Broad Bay.

The Cape Henry House today serves as the quarters of the garrison commander at Fort Story. Built in 1918 as a weather station, it served in that capacity until 1969, when the weather service relocated to Norfolk. During World War II, the building served as a Harbor Entrance Control Post for the navy and army. There are a number of ghost stories associated with this sturdy and imposing structure.

The U.S. Navy Parachute team is commonly called the Leap Frogs. The Leap Frogs traditionally perform at events throughout the country. This jump was made as a part of the demonstration for the UDT-SEAL Reunion at Fort Story in the summer 2002. A typical Leap Performance consists of 14 jumpers jumping from an aircraft at an altitude of 12,500 feet. (Courtesy Garrison Commander, Fort Story.)

These are examples of two of the insertion methods used by Navy SEALs. First the CH-47 helicopter (above) drops low over the water and the men exit the rear of the aircraft directly into the water. This exercise is called a "rubber duck" if a rubber boat is dropped from the rear of the helicopter into the water before the SEAL enters the water. If there is no boat dropped, the exercise is called a "helo cast." SEALs use the "fast rope" method of insertion to drop from a Blackhawk helicopter on dry land (left). It is imperative that the teams train in quick insertion and extraction methods. Fort Story provides an outstanding location for Special Operations training as it encompasses dry land venues as well as access to beaches in both the bay and the ocean. (Courtesy Garrison Commander, Fort Story.)

Parachutists from the U.S. Navy's Explosive Ordnance Disposal, Training and Evaluation Unit 2 (EODTEU 2) conduct a free-fall parachute jump at Fort Story. Note the lighthouse framed in the center of the team. Navy Explosive Ordnance Disposal (EOD) personnel have been stationed at Fort Story since 1968. The mission of EODTEU 2 is to train the Navy EOD forces and evaluate EOD tools and techniques. The unit provides essential support infrastructure to the Atlantic Fleet, Naval Forces Central Command, and other commands. The unit is the only advanced EOD training facility on the East Coast. The training area at Fort Story allows EODTEU 2 to be close to navy forces in Hampton Roads and offers training in full mission profiles. Navy EOD and Naval Special Warfare units use the facilities and compound to conduct research and development for tools, tactics, and procedures. The unit also provides air operations training and logistical mission support to navy EOD units. (Courtesy EODTEU 2.)

This robot is used by EOD technicians to detect and render safe improvised explosive devices (IED) in a combat theater. EODTEU 2 provides advanced training for personnel who are deploying overseas. The robot has a remote camera on top to detect an IED and a disrupting tool to render it safe. (Courtesy EODTEU 2.)

The 18th Field Hospital is a U.S. Army Reserve unit that relocated to Fort Story in 1995. Recently it moved from the wooden World War II buildings to a new Army Reserve Center. The 504-bed hospital provides support at the Army Corps and Theater levels. The hospital has deployed soldiers in support of missions in Kosovo, Iraq, Kuwait, and Afghanistan. (Courtesy 18th Field Hospital.)

The U.S. Marine Corps operates the Amphibious Reconnaissance School in a former Nike missile radar site on the beach. The facility has recently been expanded to accommodate the approximately 200 students per year who attend the school. The mission of the school is to train and teach Marines and Allied reconnaissance personnel in the skills, knowledge, tactics, and techniques of a basic recon Marine. The school is the only one of its kind on the East Coast, and the unique location at Fort Story provides immediate access to both land and water training areas. Training is conducted in patrolling, land navigation, recon and surveillance techniques, amphibious entry, and extraction, in addition to beach amphibious reconnaissance. (Courtesy *Daily Press*.)

One of the missions of the 7th Transportation Group at Fort Eustis is Joint Logistics Over the Shore (JLOTS) operations. These operations are used in areas where ports do not exist or are insufficient for military use and include the loading and unloading of strategic ships. In this 2004 exercise, a Stryker combat vehicle is driven ashore on a causeway pier built by the 331st Transportation Company. (Courtesy Public Affairs Office, Fort Story.)

In this photograph taken during the 2004 JLOTS exercise, a roll-on/roll-off discharge facility is tied to the primary vessel offshore. The cargo is then moved to the causeway pier by army or navy landing craft. This theater support vessel (TSV) represents the next generation of army watercraft and affords rapid intra-theater transport of ready-to-fight combat forces together with their equipment. (Courtesy Public Affairs Office, Fort Story.)

The 11th Transportation Battalion (Terminal) moved to Fort Story from Fort Eustis in 1979 and has served as the principal port operations unit on post since that time. The battalion had prior combat credits in World War II and Vietnam. The battalion went to Haiti and in 2003 deployed in support of Operation Iraqi Freedom. The battalion is comprised of four transportation companies. (Courtesy 11th Transportation Battalion.)

The 368th Transportation Company used the Rough Terrain Cargo Handler during cargo transfer operations in Iraq. Other equipment utilized included forklifts, 40-ton cranes, and the heavy equipment transporter. The 200 soldiers of the company were under a Corps Support Battalion and operated in the area of Baghdad, Fallujah, and Tikrit. This was the second deployment of the company in support of Operation Iraqi Freedom. (Courtesy Erik Hilberg.)

The 368th Transportation Company conducted cargo transfer operations in a large area of Iraq. Platoons of the company were in support of the 1st Marine Expeditionary Force, 1st Armored Division, 1st Infantry Division, and the 1st Cavalry Division. The company moved food, bottled water, and tons of containers and other supplies over the road in addition to forklift and crane operations. (Courtesy Erik Hilberg.)

The 368th Transportation Company returned to Fort Story in February 2005 after a year of supporting cargo operations in Iraq. The company was originally constituted in 1944 and served in the Pacific Theater during World War II. The company was also deployed to the Republic of Vietnam, where it saw extended service. The company later participated in operations in Southwest Asia, where it was awarded the Meritorious Unit Commendation (Army). (Courtesy Erik Hilberg.)

Virginia Beach
2007
400th Anniversary
Landing of the first English settlers in America

— Constance Fahey —

In 2006 and 2007, America will commemorate the settling of Jamestown, the first permanent English settlement in North America, in 1607. Jamestown established a culture that would flourish and leave the legacies of free enterprise, rule of law, representative government, and cultural interaction. Jamestown 2007 is working with over 100 local and state groups to produce a memorable commemoration. Signature events are scheduled starting in 2006 leading up to the 400th anniversary. Virginia Beach will play an active role in the activities, as the city council has established the Virginia Beach 2007 group, which is presently defining the role to be played by the community. To date, the 2007 group has organized and reached out to many organizations to make the April 2007 event worthy of the city and Hampton Roads.

ABOUT THE AUTHOR

Fielding Lewis Tyler, born in Norfolk and raised in Virginia Beach, graduated from Norfolk Academy and, following the footsteps of his father, from the Virginia Military Institute. He graduated with a bachelor of arts degree in history and was commissioned in the U.S. Army as a second lieutenant in the infantry.

After a number of years in the business world, he came on active duty at Fort Gordon, Georgia, where he commanded a basic training company. After attending school at Fort Bragg, he served as an advisor to the Vietnamese Army in the Mekong Delta area of Vietnam. Tyler returned to a later assignment at Fort Benning, Georgia, followed by an ROTC tour in Puerto Rico. He then served with the 4th Infantry Division in the Central Highlands of Vietnam. After an assignment with the Third Army in Atlanta, he returned to Vietnam for a third tour and was assigned as a briefing officer with the Military Assistance Command.

Lieutenant Colonel Tyler's career continued with an assignment to the U.S. Army Training and Doctrine Command at Fort Monroe, Virginia. After a number of years, he transferred to Germany, where he served with the Frankfurt Military Community. His final tour was at Aberdeen Proving Ground, where he retired after 30 years of service. Among his awards and decorations are the Combat Infantry Badge, Bronze Star with Combat V, Bronze Star, Legion of Merit, Joint Service Commendation Medal, Air Medal with second award, Meritorious Service Medal, Army Commendation with Two Awards, and the Republic of Vietnam Cross of Gallantry with Palm.

Lieutenant Colonel and Mrs. Tyler returned to Virginia Beach in 1989, and he was selected to be on the board of directors of the Old Coast Guard Station. He later accepted the position of executive director and currently serves in that position. He is married to the former Mary Christian Sallé. They have two daughters, Elizabeth Mathis of Phoenix and Courtenay Vass of Greensboro, North Carolina. They have three granddaughters and a dog, Ashley Muffin.

Lieutenant Colonel Tyler is a member of the Company of Military Historians and the Coast Defense Study Group. He has served on a number of boards in Virginia Beach. He has a lifelong interest in military and local history. His research and documentation have resulted in his first publication. (Photograph by Liz Tyler Mathis.)